D0387658

little
stone

James Wanless

ELEMENT
Boston, Massachusetts • Shaftesbury, Dorset
Melbourne, Victoria

© Element Books, Inc. 1999
Text © James Wanless 1999

First published in the USA in 1999 by
ELEMENT BOOKS, INC.
160 North Washington Street,
Boston, Massachusetts 02114

Published in Great Britain in 1999 by
Element Books Limited
Shaftesbury, Dorset SP7 8BP

Published in Australia in 1999 by
Element Books Limited for
Penguin Books Australia Limited
487 Maroondah Highway, Ringwood, Victoria 3134

Library of Congress Cataloging-in-Publication Data
Wanless, James.
Little stone : your friend for life / James Wanless. -- 1st ed.
p. cm. (alk. paper)
1. Divination. 2. Stone--Miscellanea. 3. Self-actualization
(Psychology)--Miscellanea. I. Title.
BF1779.S74W36   1999
133.3'22--dc21   99-19458
CIP

British Library Cataloguing in Publication data available

Printed and bound in the United States by Quebecor

ISBN 1-86204-537-2

contents

In deep, deep acknowledgement, appreciation, and awe for the greatest forgotten and most unthanked supporter of our lives—stone.

preface

S tones have always been my
friends. When I was a
boy, they were just the
best things to play with. I
would skip them in the water,
try to hit a tree with one, or use them to test
my arm strength for baseball. I have always
collected stones. I've never come home from
a hike or the beach without a pocketful or
car full. Why? Because the artist in me loves
their beauty, their form, their color. Natural
stone monuments—canyons, deserts, and
mountains—have always called me. And it
seems like forever that I've been making art

with stones, whether it's medicine wheels or strange rock piles.

One of the greatest teachers in my life was a Guatemalan shaman named Hector. For a year, I lived with him in Palencia, outside Guatemala City, and participated in building his extraordinary temples of stone. I listened to his philosophy of the "stone way of life." For Hector, the best way to know the universe was to feel and see a collection of stones. If you wanted to be useful in the universe, the best religion was stone, because stone is energy! Stone is the highest value and ultimate measure of ourselves. Hector believed that each of us is rich in this world because we can get a stone, and become our own stone.

Little Stone is my attempt to be useful in this world—like stone—by transmitting this deeply profound, yet simple and practical, truth.

Just as a stone gets more and more refined over time and change, *Little Stone* was a work in progress for years. I was periodically turning and smoothing the manuscript, just as I would turn and smooth a stone in my hand.

And rather than do extensive research on stones or read other books about stones, I let the stone speak directly to me, and listened to what it wanted to say in this book. For me, wisdom is *in* the stone. All we need to do is hold the stone and get the message. In a way, this book is only an introduction to the real book—stone itself.

As a symbologist and human empowerment professional, I always view things as symbolic mirrors of ourselves. I use physical objects as tools for personal growth and development. My intent in this book is to give you an easy way to understand yourself and provide the natural "way of the earth" path so you can realize your gifts and talents and manifest your visions and dreams.

As an oracle maker, I always use oracles as a medium to know oneself. Stones have historically been used oracularly, as a way of seeing ourselves and getting answers and direction. One of my favorite practices is "stonecasting" with my own Little Stone. I use the stone as a divinatory tool for getting in touch with my own divinity and for generating my intuitive truth on questions I may have. See Part Two to learn how to use your stone for specific oracle games.

But before all of this, you need to get your own stone. To me, this is one of the most exciting parts of the whole process. It gives you the opportunity to play the mythic role of the "shaman gatherer," and to practice the timeless, universal steps for finding what you seek; and to do so in a way different than what you have been taught and are accustomed to in this contemporary culture. See Part One to learn about this "stone way" of discovery and how you can find your own Little Stone.

All in all, there is just something magical, profoundly simple, and heartwarming in finding a friend for life in a little stone. It's hard to put into words except to say that it feels good and it feels right. Over the years, I have come to value and cherish what gives me this feeling. It is special, perhaps an opening to the soul, and, for sure, a way to the heart and to love. I hope you will feel the same.

Carmel, California
August 19, 1998

introduction

Little Stone is about the power of stone and how it will help you get in touch with the power that is within you. Little Stone, itself, is the generic name given to any stone you can hold in your hand. This book shows you how to find your own Little Stone and how it can be your friend for life. Your Little Stone will support you faithfully and without conditions. It will guide you, soothe you, energize and empower you.

Little Stone gives you an entry into the venerable art of "touch and know." The

words in this book are the thinking mind's way of explaining
the truth of being, which is
really the unspoken feeling of
being in touch. But words are like
stones: they can awaken us and help us
remember what we have forgotten.
Reconnected with our truth, we are remembered and made whole again. The teaching
of Little Stone is to remind us of what we
already know.

So many of us have lost touch with the
earth and with our sense of touch. Because
of that, we have gotten out of touch with the
real core, the real foundation, of our lives. A
stone is a powerful piece of
natural teaching that we
can easily and simply get
in touch with both physi-
cally and symbolically.

The teachings of Little Stone will give you principles to live by. These gifts from earth are the groundwork—the values—for a successful life, enduring relationships, and productive work.

Being "like a rock" in our relationships brings stability, integrity, support, and unity. Stone warns us to be open, flexible, and soft, for otherwise we risk a closed heart of stone. For lasting commitment, stone is a powerful bonding symbol. My partner and I have found a stone that represents our relationship; it sits prominently in our home as a constant reminder of our steadfast resolve to stay in touch with what holds us together.

Stone is a great advisor in business. It tells us to stay grounded, be practical, get things done and done well, to go over and over each task

until the rough edges are smoothed and the
job feels complete. My Little Stone reminds
me to produce, manifest, materialize; make
things happen in physical fact, but to be
patient. Holding my stone
helps me get focused and
centered. When I'm
unsure, Little Stone grounds
me and I return to rock solid.

In touch with stone, we get connected to
our forgotten but most primordial need—
home. Stone is home. We live on it, this
stone home we call Earth. We are born
from it, we stand on it, we die on it. We eat
from it. We are protected by its
magnetic force. We are connected to it every moment of
our lives. It contains the power
that energizes our life. It cradles
the oceans.

We use stone for all sorts of purposes—
roads, homes, fortresses, cathedrals,
tools, walls, fire pits and sacred
monuments like Stonehenge
and the Great Pyramid. We
sculpt exquisite art from it,
and use it for sacred ceremonies.

When you think about it, even our bones
are like stones.

And yet we forget. We take stone for
granted. But stones are sacrosanct, for without them, simply put, we do not exist.

Without conscious connection to stone,
we are pathologically disconnected with
ourselves. It's impossible to be genuinely
happy and healthy when we are separated
from our ultimate home base. Much of our
modern angst is the result of artificial living. As natural beings, we need nature.
Touch a stone and you return to nature, and

to your own true nature. This
is how we can heal our
heart, calm our mind, reju-
venate our body, and rekin-
dle our spirit.

You may want to find your
Little Stone right away before reading on.
If so, look at "How to Find Your Little
Stone," in Part One, *Discovery*. Then hold
your stone as you read through the rest of
the book to learn how to use it, and to
become familiar with its many qualities as
presented in Part Three, *The Story*.

Or, you may want to read *Little Stone* in
its entirety before beginning the search for
your own stone. The book will guide you in
what to look for in finding your stone and
will give you a deeper appreciation and
understanding of stones and, in particular,
your own little stone.

Stones speak to us through touch, so each chapter in Part Three, *The Story,* reveals what you get from holding and rubbing your little touchstone. Touching your Little Stone will give you physical pleasure and an emotional sense of peace and fulfillment. As a symbol of personal qualities and spiritual virtues, Little Stone gets you in touch with yourself so that you know who you are and where you are going.

part one

adventure

how to find your little stone

First and most importantly, this is an adventure—not a job, not a task, not an assignment, not something you *have* to or *should* do, but something that is fun yet challenging; new, different, and full of mystery; tiring but energizing; meaningful and magical . . . fulfilling.

Finding your stone is a great learning process, and it's exciting. In searching for the *small*, we can gain insight into the *big*. We look at the microcosm to understand the macrocosm.

In your search for Little Stone, you can learn that treating *all* of life—your work, your relationships—as adventure makes a world of difference in your well-being and in your success. Particularly when things go bad or become chaotic, facing life as an adventure, rather than as a *problem*, makes it much easier to manage.

Finding your stone is not just an adventure, but a sacred venture. Discovering yourself by discovering a symbol of yourself is a sacred mission, a spiritual path of seeking deeper wisdom and meaning. There is nothing more sacred than the pursuit of purpose and truth. Everything we do and all that we seek, in fact, give us clues and insight into our true nature. Our work and our relationships are spiritual journeys of self-discovery—and our

lives would be greatly enhanced and elevated by having this perspective.

Finding your Little Stone is a mythic and archetypal sacred adventure. You act out the role of the "gatherer," seeking to gather to you what you seek. It's unlike the "hunter," which has been the prevailing male-style of getting something. Gathering is gentle, peaceful, feminine, shamanic. In gathering your stone you are like a medicine woman or medicine man, looking for something that will heal and transform you. The old, predatory way will sooner or later make you the prey: the hunter becomes the hunted. Gathering, in contrast, creates a gathering, a community, a team.

Gathering good medicine requires using the power of attraction. Let Little Stone come to you by allowing yourself to be drawn to a certain area in a certain direction at a certain time. It's like this: a great baseball hitter lets the pitch come to him and then goes *with* the pitch, hits it in the direction the ball itself wants to go.

You do this by letting go and following the force that magnetizes you. Open your senses to the joy of adventure. Open up your breath and breathe in the nature; breathe in the scents and sounds. Open your eyes and see the colors and the clouds. Rub your hands on a tree and dig your feet into the sand and into the earth. Hum, whistle, and sing; talk to the river, the flowers, and the mushrooms.

Getting out of your normal mind-state, you are natural. When you are at one with nature, it will lead you. Don't think, don't judge. Let the natural impulse of your open sense of curiosity take you along.

This is easy but difficult—it runs so counter to our way of making things happen through the force of our personal egoic will. To be open, attentive, and moving in harmony with an invisible pull and vibration is the path of happiness and genius. Forcing, striving, and driving leads to stress, burnout, and limited solutions.

In this way the stone itself naturally suggests how it wants to be approached.

Allowing your stone to find you in a situation of mystery—of not knowing where or what, of not having a map— is an intuitive process. In the dark, we can go only with a feeling, an intuition. And intuition is not a skill we are taught. When we look for something, we usually research how to do it, we ask for directions, we depend on hard information. There is no such possibility in seeking your stone. Little Stone is personal to you; there is no rhyme or reason why it should be here or there, or what it should even look like. Your own inner voice, vision, or feeling is what you must follow. And in this world of uncertainty—of rapid change and multiple possibilities—intuition is the only way to make correct decisions. Study after study has shown that following a gut feeling or hunch is the way successful people communicate and work.

In Little Stone, what you are seeking is a friend, a friend for life. The stone that comes to you must feel like a friend. What a wonderful and unusual thing it is to find such a lifelong friend, a friend that will always accept you just as you are, who asks nothing of you, who, if you ask, will give you excellent advice, who will always make you feel better, and who will never leave you unless you leave it.

Befriending Little Stone, we learn what true friendship is. Usually we look for people who can help us or who we can help, or for someone we just like, or to make a friend of somebody who just happens to be around. If we were to apply the principles of our friendship with Little Stone to our human friends, we would have a whole different level of relationship with more caring, more love, more fun, more creativity, and more growth. If we could be like a Little Stone friend to others, the world would be a much better place.

Remember, your Little Stone is a friend.
It doesn't have to be a pretty stone, a color-
ful stone, a valuable stone, or any kind of
particular stone. It must be only your stone,
and it must come into your hands direct
from nature. We are so used to only valuing
that which has been polished, or cut, or
determined as our birthstone, or those stones
considered powerful or expensive or rare.
And we are accustomed to acquiring these
things through commercial retail. Your
truest friend cannot be bought and doesn't
have to be good-looking or successful. It
must be a natural meeting without interme-
diary. In our world we are so
impressed by the beautiful,
by the rich and famous.
True friendship comes
with no pretension, no
hype, no credentials, no

projection of who I want to be, and who I want to impress. If we were to look for such genuine friendships in our relation-ships, business partnerships, and social lives, we would be happier, more successful and more fulfilled.

When you do find your Little Stone ask, as you hold it, what you can learn from it. Ask clearly and simply, "Please Little Stone, what do you have to teach me?" As you feel the stone, the thought or thoughts that arise are your answer. Another way to ask the question might be, "How can I grow from hav-ing you, Little Stone, in my life?" The key is to trust whatever comes immedi-ately to mind. Do not discount an idea that is quick, simple, and easy—these are your most important intuitive insights.

Every meeting in our lives happens for a higher purpose; every meeting is a chance for evolution. We should always ask ourselves how we can grow from our associations and friendships. This makes our connections and partnerships far more meaningful and empowering.

Any friendship or relationship must be taken care of so it can grow and endure. How should you care for your Little Stone? At the very least, put it in a distinctive place so that you won't lose it. The more you treat your stone as a special entity, the more impact it will have on your life. We have a tendency in our lives to make things mundane, as just commonplace and ordinary. If we treat our relations as special, they will be extraordinary and highly valuable.

Remember the keys to finding and
befriending your Little Stone:

- *Treat it as an adventure.*
- *Know that it is sacred.*
- *Be a gatherer.*
- *Follow the power of attraction.*
- *Use your intuition.*
- *Look for a friend for life.*
- *Let it happen naturally.*
- *Ask what you can learn
  from your stone.*
- *Take special care of it.*

part two

discovery

how to use this book and your
little stone

Little Stone is not
your customary
book. It's a multi-
functional, inter-dimen-
sional self-discovery tool,
a book of spiritual wis-
dom, a guide to personal
growth, *and* an ancient oracle.

As a wisdom book, *Little Stone* offers a
universal set of principles to live by. Each of
the 24 "chapters" presents a spiritual eco-
psychology for living a more natural, earth-
principled life.

Somewhat of a nat-
ural drama, *Little
Stone* is also a story
about the life of a
stone. As such, it's a
soft science text on the history and evolution of rock and earth. My own Little Stone
that inspired this book was the geological
basis for this story. Your own stone may
have a somewhat different earth history. If,
like a scientist, you seek out the origin and
the history of your stone, you will uncover a
hole in time that connects us with our pre-
human ancestry and elemental foundations.
This investigation of our time and space in
the universe will give you an expanded
sense of self-identity, community, and
home.

But on its deepest level, the primary
function of this book to provide you with an

instructional and experiential handbook so
you can learn how to use a stone for your
own self-development.

Little Stone is an actual ritual of
befriendment, a sacred process of
finding, keeping, and nurturing
unconditional love and friendship. Over the course of years,
I have collected many Little
Stones that were special to me
and have given them to friends in exchange
for their *own* Little Stone. This exchanging
creates a bonding that lasts. It preserves ties
that overcome time, differences, and space.
Try it.

Stone wisdom show you how to live your
life from the point of view of a rock. This
may seem laughable, but stone represents
many principles and qualities that are necessary and timely for ourselves in this mod-

ern world. In our speeding life of relativity,
I find it very comforting to have a solid set
of principles that don't change from
moment to moment and from viewpoint to
viewpoint. As life accelerates into a blur,
those who have a core set of values to
live by will be valued. Stability,
reliability, practicality, and sim-
plicity are stone-sure imperatives
for managing the momentum of
the new millennium.

Each of the short chapters in the Story of
Little Stone illuminates an empowering
characteristic of stone that reflects our own
strength to survive and evolve. Use these
insights and principles to know more about
yourself and to guide your life.

Better yet, express these principles in
your life. *Little Stone* is primarily a handbook for how to apply in real life the wis-

dom of the Little Stone that you find. You
can use *Little Stone* as an action plan-
ner, for the chapters present a map
and formula for following the
principles of stone to get rock
solid in your business and grounded in your relationships.

As you read through the
story of the generic stone
called Little Stone, it
gives you *italicized* directions for handling your
stone to cultivate in you the qualities of
stone that are essential in guiding, healing,
transforming, and empowering ourselves.
These "touchstone" exercises are reminders.
They get us in touch with the down-to-
earth attributes we often forget about in
ourselves. In all cases, these insights are
physically felt in your hands.

I originally called *Little Stone* a "touch and know" book, for the real book is the stone in your hand. Touch it, observe what you feel, and learn something about yourself. Books are abstracted metaphors from real life; this one, if you get the stone, is physically real. To literally feel the message and feel the truth is unique and powerful. Knowing through the primary sense of touch is cellular and primal, impossible to dismiss and indelibly memorable. This sensory, non-mental approach to self-discovery activates intuitive knowing, our deepest and most authentic voice and self.

Do the touch and know processes, and by doing, I mean take action on your intuitive insights. Stone is a physical fact, so to follow the stone teachings, take actions that can be physically evidenced. The stone path is a manifestation practice, so it's about material-

izing what's in your heart, soul, and mind.
This book was written by adhering to the
qualities of my own Little Stone. Simply
having the stone visible and touchable gave
me the inspiration to get the book done!
The stone principles in the chapters on
Energy, Grounding, Creativity, Wholeness,
and Legacy particularly guided me in pro-
ducing this work.

Little Stone is an active and productive
self-help therapy, a stepping-stone process.
For each of the 24 chapters or steps
on the Little Stone journey of
life, take a step—do something,
and then continue on to the
next step. And then do the steps
again, repeating the process, for the
secret to success is repetition, going over
and over, around and around, then and only
then is perfection attained. Why is it that

the sun rises and sets every day? So that we have enough opportunity to get it right.

I continually go back to the quality of stone discussed in the first chapter, called Journey. It reminds me that life—everything in life—is a journey. With that constantly in mind, I have become much more purposeful and intentional in my life. I have become more adaptable to change, more able to move along with events and to see how those events can turn me around. I am more on my toes now about possible opportunities and pitfalls along the way, and I can see how those setbacks are a necessary and valuable part of the journey.

Stones have always been used for oracular purposes. Crystal balls, gemstones, inscriptions on rocks have all served as ways of divining people's destinies. You can use your little stone as a medium for pulling out intuitions, visions, and voices from within you. A stone is neutral, full of mystery and wisdom of the ages, perfect for eliciting extraordinary perception. And *Little Stone* can function as a set of interpretations and commentary for playing with your stone as an oracle game.

There are several ways of playing oracle with your stone. Hold and rub your Little Stone with your eyes closed as you visualize the stone in your mind's eye. This gives you a neutral, blank open space into which your intuition can come forth. In this open state, what question arises for you? Ask it aloud. The question, itself, may be the insight you have been seek-ing, for often the questions we ask contain hidden within them an answer. But

listen also for the answer that comes to you.
The essential principle is to let Little Stone
be a vehicle, a focusing point, to trigger
your own intuition. As you touch and look
at (or visualize) the stone, it will evoke from
your subconscious a rock-based piece of
information that surfaces in a variety of
ways. The answer is the first thing that
comes to you, whether it be a picture in
your mind, a symbol, a word, a whole set of
ideas, a voice, a feeling, a sense—whatever.
For an answer to have validity, it must ring
true in some way to you.

The more often you consult your Little
Stone, the easier this process of question-
and-answer will become. It can evolve into
a kind of "oracular conversation," in which
you muse with your stone-muse to reflect
on and contemplate the issues in your life.

You might want to try the game of

"stone casting." Draw a set of 24 circles in the ground or in sand, each numbered for one of the 24 chapters in the Little Stone story. Throw your stone over your shoulder or with your eyes closed. Your answer is cast by the circle it falls in.

A more elaborate stone casting game is to gather 24 stones, each one representing one of the 24 Little Stone qualities. The collection process is, of itself, a powerful oracular process that requires intention, intuition, instinct. And you can have meaningful fun making a bag for your stones. With these stones, throw them out, and try to discern what sort of symbolic pattern they make, and interpret or "read" this stone cast. Another version of this is to cast the stones and see which one is most alone or furthest away from all the others. This "outcast" stone is the one to read, for it stands out and begs attention.

Even another way of reading the stones is to cast them out and see which ones seem to stay close to one another. A colleague of mine did this and noticed that two stones were always in contact. One of the stones represented her risk-taking, her do-some-thing-different side (the "Stepping Stone": Change), and the other stone her highest, wisest, and truest self (the "Crone Stone": Wisdom). That they were together indicated to her that it was time to take an outlandish adventure and, in so doing, discover a deeper and more profound truth about herself. Off to India she went, and has come back forever changed.

I particularly enjoy the process of stacking the

25

stones on top of each other, as high as I can, without letting them fall. It's interesting to see which stones must go on top or below another in order to support the tower. This structure can have symbolic meaning. For example, I noticed that the "Father Stone" (Protection) was naturally comfortable and well-placed above my "Specialness Stone." I read this oracle as a message to me to guard, value, and use my special and unique gifts.

Remember, however, that no answer is ever "cast in stone." Things change; people change; situations change. Stonecasts are, in fact, catalysts for change. Draw in the information and move on, like a rolling stone.

part three

the story

1

JOURNEY

The Little Stone

LITTLE STONE GOT HER NAME because she's so small. But really not so little; she's had a big, big life. In fact, Little Stone has lived a life much larger than yours. She's older than you, in some ways stronger than you, more stable and peaceful than you, and perhaps even more true to herself.

~~~

Little Stone is so old that over the years in the journey of life she has had many different names and many different adventures. This is her story. It is about all the many kinds of stone she has been and all the qualities she has shown throughout her life.

It's most important to know that written within *her* story is our own life story. Who she has been and what she is becoming reveal to us our own qualities and opportunities as we journey through life.

We begin the story by letting our little friend and guide take us back to the beginning.

When you hold your Little Stone, you are holding the history of this Earth. She goes back in time and she will go ahead in time. Touching her, you are in touch with the journey of life. Know also that you've

*had a long life now behind you, and have a
long life yet to come.*

*So when you don't like the way things are
going in your life, get moving. Think different.
Journey on. And when you want things to
remain just the way they are, be ready to let
go, for life will not remain the same. Life is
like a wheel of fortune: you will have ups and
downs. So ride the life voyage by keeping to
the center, to the middle point of balance.*

*Hold Little Stone to center you in the
present, between the past and future, the com-
ings and goings, the highs and lows.*

2

ENERGY

The Fire Stone

IN THE BEGINNING, LITTLE STONE was not a stone but a swirling mass of gas and fire. Born as red hot molten lava from the inside core of Mother Earth, she was poured from the very same primal energy of liquid light that gave birth to our planet.

Gradually, Little Stone cooled and became hardened fire. She took form and became a great mountain. In her original majesty, she was like an Earth all on her own. In holding this once great rock, you touch the elemental power of creation.

Little Stone is energy, like a small battery that charges you. It gives you life just like this stone called Earth. Everything in life comes down to energy. Without it, nothing happens, nothing works, nothing lives. Wouldn't it be nice to have more energy? Little Stone can give you that boost. It's subtle but effective.

Hold Little Stone as a personal energizer. Rub it with each hand to power both sides of your body, the left that brings in energy and the right that puts out energy.

Rub it on the soles of your feet to give you spring in your step, and touch it to the top of your head to let it ground you.

Fully charged, take charge of your life and charge ahead.

3

CONNECTION

The Touch Stone

JUST LIKE US, LITTLE STONE WAS transformed from raw energy into physical matter. From the ineffable breath of life, we became living, physical beings. The track back to our first transformation into material form takes us to our core. Here, our path of human life begins . . . from soil to soul, from humus to human.

~~~

In this physical life, our first knowing is touch. The sense of touch is our original intelligence. In the womb, we saw with touch, we heard with touch, we tasted with touch.

The modern emotional and spiritual dis-ease is separation. We have lost touch with one another and with nature and, most importantly, with ourselves, with our own soul. Our sickness of spiritual disconnection is not cured by exotic solutions but by a return to the simplest, most natural and pri-mary source of connection—physical touch.

Touch is the soul's first kiss.

Touch a stone and you get in touch with the origin of life. Little Stone is a portal to knowing where you have come from and who you are. As you touch Little Stone, you are in touch with this Earth home of ours and in touch with yourself.

When you are feeling disconnected, alone, out of touch with yourself or others . . . touch the stone. You will begin to know and feel connected, to be in union with the world and yourself.

Perhaps at first, you won't feel much. That's because we have been so out of touch for so long. Keep touching, keep rubbing, keep holding. Again and again and again, stay in contact.

4

GROUNDING

The Earth Stone

OUT OF ORIGINAL MATTER, LITTLE
Stone became the very ground we stand on,
the stone called Earth. But instead of
accepting our down-to-earth nature, all of
us are flying about, always looking, trying
to find fulfillment of some kind or another.
We are all on a quest for the grail of our

choice. But the harder we search for it, the more elusive it often becomes; we seem to get even busier and more stressed. Have you noticed that we are moving faster and faster, achieving more and more, and are yet often less fulfilled?

We don't find whatever it is we are seeking because we have forgotten the first thing—the stone home on which we base our whole lives, which literally supports us. The ground. As our foundation, stone has guiding wisdom, it gives us the essential ingredients for successful living. Back to the basics, the fundamentals, we find our way to happiness.

Why don't we see it? Because it's too obvious. Because we are too busy standing on it. Because we take it so much for granted and never give it any thought. Or per-

haps because we are too much in our
thoughts to even notice.

Just as this world spins around, turn
your own head around. Go to the bottom to
get to the top. The secret is right under
your feet. The stone on which you stand
and sit and rest and breathe is the first
thing, the homebase where everything
begins and ends.

*To heal yourself of anxiety and
        addictions . . .
To calm the feverish, endless yearning
        for more, new and different . . .
To be at peace, fulfilled . . .
To accept what is and be happy . . .*

*Ground Yourself . . .
Touch the stone.*

5

POWER

The Magnet Stone

AS THE BEDROCK OF EARTH, LITTLE
Stone became very powerful. In her is the
power of magnetism, that force which
keeps us and everything together.

Although Little Stone is small, she is
mighty . . . she attracted my attention. We
are magnetized by her. She has a hold on

us, luckily, or we would go flying off into space. As a magnet, she's full of power to attract, influence, and hold.

No matter how small or insignificant you may think you are, you have the power of stone. Your body is magnetic, regardless of what it looks like. Even more magnetizing is your life vitality. Full of concentrated fire and energy, you are compelling and attractive.

Let Little Stone empower you. Hold her and remember your own magnetism. You have the power to attract and hold attention. You don't have to try so hard to be liked, to be loved, to be influential. It's natural.

Use your power wisely, for you will bring to you what you put out. Like attracts like. So be happy and you will bring happiness into your life. Be loving and have love. Smile and bring joy to you. Share your gifts and you will be gifted.

6

WISDOM

The Crone Stone

LITTLE STONE HAS COME A LONG
way into your hands—a journey of eons and
eons. She's a crone, an ancient elder, a grand-
mother. In fact, this little rock is our oldest
and wisest connection to our beginnings on
Earth. Making connection with our ancestor
in this little old stone, we remember who we
are and who we have been.

~~~

Guardian of the past, this rock of ages
also carries a song, a call to life everlasting.
Listen to it. It's ironic that in this aged stone
is found the way back to youth. For in the
little crone we can go back in time, and by
its time-tested experience, know how to
endure and go forward.

Life these days is all about keeping up,
being able to change and grow. How to do
this? Who can show us?

*Touch Little Stone and touch your
past. Refined by time, you are wise. In
your bones, the bodystone, you carry
billions of years of wisdom. As you squeeze
Little Stone, close your eyes and hum along
with her, and feel into your past. How many
places have you come from? How many
changes have you made? How many crises*

have you survived? How many times have you begun again?

Know that your life is rock wise, based on more experience than you have probably ever imagined. Touch the stone and consult the Crone within you for advice about anything, for how to survive in our topsy-turvy world.

HOME

Mother Stone

AS FIRST MATTER, STONE IS OUR MA, our mother. Out of stone we have emerged, so it's true in a way: Little Stone is our mother. Just imagine how many human, animal, and plant births she has supported. As the mother of all mothers, the Mother Stone makes us feel secure, at home. She gives of herself with unconditional love, always reliable and dependable. So strong and yet so soft. Through her, we grow our roots and wings . . . so that we can fly, knowing we can return to her. She is home base, always there for us.

Haven't we all felt at times insecure, dis-located, unsure, foreign, maybe even alien? Without a sense of place—home—there can be no peace, no comfort, no security, no rest. Feeling at home is the base, ground zero for happiness and success in life.

When you are feeling insecure, uncomfortable, homeless, hold your Little Mother Stone. Hold it and know that you are home. You are safe, confi-dent, strong, and supported. In the hold of Mother Earth, you can be at peace, Relax, rest assured.

8

PROTECTION

The Father Stone

LIFE FOR LITTLE STONE HAS SELDOM been boring. She has been thrust out from the center of the Earth, buried in the dark, crushed by boulders, fallen off cliffs, seared and scorched by the sun, tumbled down raging rivers, and thrown asunder by giant ocean waves.

Despite these countless tumbles and falls, Little Stone has survived, protected because she is rock hard. Very little can violate or destroy her and her fortress stone citadel.

Stone is like our father, a knight protector. It steadfastly protects us from the fires, the winds, the waters, and the intruders.

How often do we feel unprotected, open and exposed to the wild world about us? To survive in this modern concrete jungle, we must build rock hard boundaries and defend ourselves against intrusions and invasions.

As you hold tight the Little Father Stone, know in its hardness that you, too, have the muscle and concentrated inner strength to deter any threat to your well-being. When you feel endangered by outside

forces, grab your stone and resolve your will.
Compact and close yourself off. Let nothing
get in. Be a fortress of stone.

Let this little Father Stone be your shield,
even a weapon of defense, a projectile that
could save your life.

9

INTEGRITY

The Core Stone

LITTLE STONE'S HARDNESS COMES from her inner core of cohesiveness created by a conscious sense of herself as a stone, to which she holds hard and steadfast. This inner unity is her *integrity*, an inner core of knowing who she is. Being true to her stone nature keeps her whole and healthy to the core.

Our own weaknesses come from not having a strong sense of self. We are depleted by parts of ourself that criticize and undermine us, that don't value and hold esteem for who we are. How often have we negated and compromised ourselves? How often have we torn ourselves down and crushed our own aspirations and abilities because we don't believe in ourselves?

If you tend to sabotage yourself through low self-esteem, hold Little Stone. Hold rock hard to who you are, to your values, your truth and integrity, and to your self-value.

In touch with the core of this Earth and your own core, you have the strength and unity within yourself to be as magnificent as this wondrous earth.

10

COMMONNESS

The Family Stone

OVER THE COURSE OF HUNDREDS
and hundreds of thousands of years, Little
Stone has gradually been worn down as a
mountain and has joined the great common
ground.

Although Little Stone, as you see her
now, is all alone, that's not really true. As a

stone, she is still part of the mother stone. Little Stone is united with all the other little and large stones in the world. Little Stone is part of one great big family of stone.

Sometimes we feel so small and isolated, alone. But we are not. Like Little Stone, we belong to a much, much larger community of life. We are part of a great family.

Little Stone's commonness reminds us of our own commonness. Like so many other stones, she's a small fragment of the great common, as are we. Each of us is common because we hold so much in common with others. What we feel is what others feel. Knowing this, you'll never feel alone again.

And sometimes when you feel higher or lower than others, let Little Stone remind you of your place as a common person, just like others.

Whenever you feel alone and want to get in touch with others, touch your Little Stone friend and get in touch with your own big family. We are all in this together, one family, for no thing and no one is alone. When you get in touch with the family stone, know that you have friends and a support group that is always there. There is a common ground of mutual understanding. If you want something from another, ask for it and you will be heard, for you are not uncommon.

11

SPECIALNESS

Your Own Stone

THE MOST COURAGEOUS STEP EVER taken by Little Stone was to break away and break out into her own, to be her own stone. This was not easy. To leave her family and become a stone unto herself was painful yet exhilarating. In breaking off, she became free, free to go her own way and carve out her own life.

So, although Little Stone is related and similar to every other stone, she has become unique and special, unlike any other stone.

Sometimes we feel so ordinary, but really we are distinctive in our own way. But to find our individuality we must break off to follow our own path. Just as Little Stone did: to let go and detach from the hold of our mother, father, and family is a natural step of life.

 When you have lost touch with your own specialness, which is being out of touch with yourself, touch Little Stone and reclaim your originality. Set yourself free to be the distinctive and uncommon person that you are. Let Little Stone remind you of the journey you have taken to become yourself. You are your own stone. You are special.

12

CREATIVITY

The Creation Stone

TO BECOME HER OWN STONE, LITTLE Stone had to create her own life. In a way, she's an artist. She has sculpted herself into the stone that you see. Her path of self-creation has been one of constantly chipping away unnecessary and outworn pieces of herself. Even right now, she is redefining

and refining herself to find her own perfect
self-expression.

Have you ever felt that you weren't creative? Well, that's not true. Each of us
designs our own destiny. Every one of us is
an artist in the way we form our lives.

Just like Little Stone, we create our lives
by the energy within us, but we are also not
the only creator. Like stone, other forces in
life are at work in shaping us. We are here
to co-create, to simultaneously seize and
surrender our creative power. Creativity
occurs by joing forces; it's time to coalesce,
combine, collaborate, team up, partner, ally.

 *When you touch Little Stone, you are
in touch with creation, and get in
touch with the creator in you.*
*Who do you want to see yourself become?
And what are you whittling away at in your*

life to be your own person in your own unique way? What are you cutting away to reveal the real you? You may need to get rid of old beliefs about yourself, or even situations that hold you back.

But also ask how you can best use the situations and energies in life that are supporting and guiding the creation of yourself. How can you effectively co-create?

The key is to take action on these questions, then you can actually materialize something new in you and your life. You make it happen by making it real. Little Stone is a physical fact, here to impress upon you the need to do it! And be patient; good things take time.

Like a stone, work hard and wait, work again and wait again.

13

VISION

The Eye Stone

LITTLE STONE HAS BEEN AROUND such a long time that she has seen it all. But she continues to look and search, for her journey of self-creation continues. She is still designing her life using her artist's eye. Little Stone is what we call a seer. Her foresight is like our own ability to make a picture of the future that creates the future. Like us, she is her own oracle.

Have you ever wanted to see things that you can't see with your physical eye? Like the future? Like new opportunities? Like what someone else is feeling? It's easy: just use your own inner vision, or imagination, and what do you see? Use your own inner intuition and what do you feel? What do you sense with your own senses?

Little Stone is really like a mirror. It helps you see what's in your own mind's eye. So what do you want to know? Like rubbing your eyes to see more clearly, rub the little stone, and you can see infinity. The universe lies within it. Little Stone is pregnant with all possibility. Look deep into it and what emerges for you? That's

what is growing within you, wanting to come
out and break free. And if you can conceive it,
you can make it.

See it and be it.

14

PEACE

The Smooth Stone

IN THE COURSE OF HER LIFE, ALL the elements of nature have at one time or another been at war with Little Stone. Other stones have tried to crush her. The waters have sought to drown her. Humans have attempted to quarry her. Soil has tried to suffocate her.

Little Stone has gone through so many ups and downs and turns of life that she has become smoothed by experience. She is at peace and nothing can upset her now. But her peacefulness has come from being bumped and worn and broken and moved.

Life is like that. We are honed and refined into a state of peace through conflict and adversity. By learning to accept this inherent state of opposition, we achieve an easy, smooth unity with it all. We are not here to fight the natural polarity and differences of life, but to get along with our competition and diversity.

Wouldn't it be nice to be at peace? To feel at ease with life, even if it's not easy? To ride the upsets and setbacks like a rolling stone. It's possible—bumps are fun!

In rubbing your smooth Little Stone, you get a sense of peace. Let this peace stone calm you down, smooth out your feelings and thoughts so you can go along and get along with adversity easily and comfortably as part of the natural ride of life.

When you are feeling angry and upset, at odds with others and life, touch your stone and feel the tranquillity and acceptance.

15

SILENCE

The Truth Stone

DURING HER LONG LIFE, LITTLE Stone has heard it all. So much so that it would be impossible to tell. And so she keeps her silence.

She has listened to the roar of cracking earth and thunder, the howling winds, the pounding thud of ocean waves, the howl of coyotes, and the clattering hooves of great moving beasts. How could she be heard surrounded by such sounds of power? By silence. By saying nothing, she says everything.

Words are like stones. Too many words become pebbles with not much impact or meaning.

Too many words become noise, static that impairs our listening. We cannot hear for the talk. Little Stone has enduring wisdom, like the unspeaking Sphinx. In her silence, she can hear the truth.

Wouldn't it be nice to have some quiet? And, in silence, know the truth, even the truth of our own inner voice? The clatter of our noisy, busy world clutters and fatigues the mind, depletes our energy, distorts and diverts us from knowing.

Whenever you need quiet and want to hear what's really going on, hold the silent Little Stone and be silent. In this meditative quiet, the truth will talk to you and you will hear.

16

SIMPLICITY

The Plain Stone

LITTLE STONE HAS, INDEED, LIVED a full and rich life, but in spite of her long travels, vast experience, and ancient wisdom, she is so simple and plain. What you see is what you get—nothing fancy, no big deal, obvious, no pretension.

Haven't you ever wanted to make your

life more simple? Our lives become so complex that *we* become complex, and all tied
up with things, obligations, etc., etc. We
have a hard time keeping it going and all
together. We get confused, complicated,
fragmented and frazzled by it all.

*Touch the simple Little Stone as a
reminder to keep your own life simple.
There's really not much to it. Just stay
true to a few simple principles:*

- *believe in yourself,*
- *follow your joy,*
- *create what you want out of life,*
- *accept what happens,*
- *and keep going.*

17

MYSTERY

The Secret Stone

FOR MILLIONS OF YEARS, LITTLE Stone has lived in secret. Her life is full of secrets. Where has she come from? What's inside of her? Only Little Stone knows.

Little Stone may seem boring to you, so plain and simple, but really there is a great inner life of constant movement, of invisible

~~~

change, going on within her. In fact, Little Stone, like all of us, is more space than stuff. Now, that's a mystery to me. And in open spaces, anything can come in and go out. So, the possibility of change always exists. Who knows what the next moment may bring?

Sometimes we think of ourselves as so ordinary, so mundane, so apparent, but in fact we are full of mystery. We are born to life out of the mystery and are returning to the great mystery again. In seeking to understand the mystery of life, we tap into the great force that gives us being. To wonder is to understand.

 When you feel like a boring, uninteresting person, touch the mystery of Little Stone and remember all the

mysterious richness within yourself. At any one moment, you are a whole complex of secret history and experience, full of feelings, sensations, thoughts, perceptions, like a veritable galaxy of atoms and things spinning and bouncing around inside of you acting and reacting.

At any time, something new can happen if you let it. All things are possible with an open and curious mind.

18

SMALLNESS

The Small Stone

ATHOUGH SHE HAS GROWN IN MANY
ways, Little Stone has become physically
smaller and smaller. Life is not about size
and stuff. It's about the life essence, the
invisible energy that makes life. Her whole
existence has been about breaking away, letting go, and releasing her mass and material

to reach this spirit essence. She is so small now because she has chipped away her ego, the desire to be big and famous, big and rich, big and shiny.

There is nothing wrong with accumulating size and stuff; just know that inevitably, as the stone rolls, life will eventually wear and refine you down to your pure essence of no matter and no thing.

Who are you anyway? How big do you think you are . . . compared to the sun and the stars?

When you are feeling small and as though you are losing it all, get in touch with the small Little Stone and be comforted in the wisdom and power of the small. Let Little Stone touch your spirit and remind you of the falsity of human arrogance and ego. It's okay not to have so much. In fact, without heaps of stuff, you are probably more in touch with the life force, and more vital, more alive, more rich.

19

HEALING

The Perfect Stone

OVER THE YEARS AS WE HAVE ALREADY
seen, Little Stone has been wounded, cut up
and pared down, run over, thrust over, cov-
ered by water, burned by heat, frozen by
night, crushed by boulders, withered and
weathered by rain and snow. But each time
that her life has been turned over and tum-

bled, she has become more and more perfect, more whole and healthy. In the wounding, she has healed herself . . . so that now she can heal you.

As you know, life can hurt. Why is it that way? Because it's part of the process of being processed, of being perfected by pain and suffering.

When you want to feel better, touch the healing stone. When you are down about life because of all its pains and hassles, setbacks and disappointments, touch Little Stone and remember that it's in the tumultuous crucible of life that you become more perfected.

Heal yourself, knowing that every wound is an opportunity for you to perfect yourself, and, in turn, heal others.

20

WHOLENESS

The Round Stone

WHAT YOU SEE AND FEEL IN LITTLE Stone are the results of an amazing circle journey of life. She has truly been around, having exprienced all the elements and seasons, the ages of fire and ice, stone and silicone, the dinosaur and back to the cavedwellers, from drought to floods, from war to peace, from villages to isolation, from creation to desolation. And, in turn, she has gone around and around on herself. By making the rounds, Little Stone has become well-rounded, or whole unto herself.

Wholly rounded, she's fully capable of taking care of herself, to be self-sufficient in any situation. Through the power of circling and circulating, Little Stone has achieved the epitome of life—completeness. She has completed the great adventure and become whole.

Our life is an inescapable journey to wholeness. We have to go around and around, and sometimes we get in a rut and begin to wonder whether it's worth it all and what the point is anyway.

*When you are bored, tired of it all,
stuck in repetition, getting nowhere
and are unfulfilled, unsatisfied,
incomplete, then feel the roundedness and
wholeness of Little Stone. Like a seed, Little
Stone plants in your consciousness the flower
of wholeness.*

*Little Stone's own completeness reminds you
to go the whole nine yards, to complete things.
What haven't you completed? By feeling her
roundedness, remember to go full circle. By
going all the way around, you finish and
become finished. And when you're really done,
then you are ready to move on, to roll into a
new revolution, a new cycle, a new turn.*

*In this way of the circle, you recycle and
renew. You move in harmony with the spiral-
ing universe. You can do no more.*

21

CHANGE

The Stepping Stone

THE LIFE OF LITTLE STONE HAS been a journey of transformation. As we know from her story, she has not remained the same. Change is a fact of life for all of us, and yet we often resist it. When we go against change, we go against life. We become stagnant, obsolete, depressed, dead.

We have each chosen to live, so change is
the path we must take.

*When you hold Little Stone, notice
how you rub it, turn it around, and
keep it moving in your hand.
Whenever you don't feel good about your life,
change the position of the stone in your hand
and remember to change your life. Take steps.
Move on.*

*As a stepping stone, Little Stone propels you
forward to the next step. Keep going, for you
are on a path, a neverending path. And Little
Stone will guide your steps on and on.*

22

NATURALNESS

The Rolling Stone

NEVER ONCE HAS LITTLE STONE departed from her nature as a rolling stone. She has accepted the ever-changing nature of life. She just rolls on and on to her next destination and beyond.

Wouldn't it be nice to do things so naturally? So much of our stress and unhappiness results from not being natural, from not rolling along with the natural revolutions of life. We think we should do this or that. We've been told how we are supposed to be and we conform. Natural living comes with no shoulds from others. We get stuck and blocked by thinking, and have forgotten how to just spontaneously *be*.

When you feel awkward, not real, as though you are playing a role, living an artificial life, not in touch with your true nature, not doing what you know is right for you, touch Little Stone and remember your nature as part of nature. Do what comes naturally. Being in touch with the earth will bring you down to earth to live the natural way.

23

SERVICE

The Philosopher's Stone

AT FIRST GLANCE, LITTLE STONE may look like a meaningless, insignificant rock, but in fact, she was created with a great purpose. Indeed, everything in this world has a reason for being.

Born to serve, Little Stone has been our life support, the soil from which we eat and

〜〜〜

the ground from which we leap. She has been a tool and the material we use to make great and small things. Little Stone gives us the minerals that fortify our bodies and bones.

Little Stone makes a philosopher of us all. She reminds us of our purpose. So often we forget why we are here. We think our lives are meaningless or that we are here to take care of only ourselves. We are here to serve, and in so doing, be served.

As you touch Little Stone, ask yourself, what does stone give to you and to the world? To have great life purpose and a deeper meaning of life, let Little Stone remind you that you, too, are like a stone, here as a gift of service to the world.

You are gifted by birth with the inherent abililty and responsibility to support, nurture, heal, and fortify yourself and others. Ask how you can help support and sustain life. How do you offer your gifts? How do you serve?

24

LEGACY

The Spirit Stone

ALL THINGS ON EARTH HAVE A message that is embedded in the vibration of their energy. We take on these energies through contact with them. Many of our difficulties in life are the result of being in contact with unhealthy energies.

Little Stone is natural, clean, and wise.

All the ways you touch and are touched by her give you good vibes. The more you contact her, the deeper you retain her messages to you. You carry her within your heart and soul and in the life you lead. You become her legacy, her gift to posterity.

Each of us leaves a legacy, a footprint on the world. How do you want to be remembered? What do you want to leave behind as your way of helping succeeding generations?

Remember that in every moment of our lives, we are sending a message by the energy we impart. Our legacy is being felt at this very time.

 If you keep rubbing your Little Stone, its virtues will rub off on you, and rub off on others as your legacy.

As you hand it down to your children and they to their children, your energy will be embodied in it and your legacy will continue . . . and Little Stone will grow in power and magic to help others as she helped you.

Over the generations, the touch-and-know story of Little Stone will go on and on . . . and she will get littler and littler . . . until she is no more. She will have completed her earth journey. But her spirit will survive in the hearts and minds and lives of our successors . . . and the great adventure will continue.

When you put away your Little Stone, do it with a prayer of "thank you."

JAMES WANLESS is the author and creator of the internationally best-selling *The Voyager Tarot*. He has a Ph.D. in political science from Columbia University. He has traveled the world studying philosophy and anthropology while training others self-mastery. He resides in Carmel, California.